Our 1st Protest

written by London Carter Williams.
illustrated by Subi Bosa

ISBN: 978-0-578-74641-8
Copyright 2020 London Carter Williams

Dedication

This book is dedicated to all my HEROES,
past and present. Here are the names of a few.
Thank you for ALL that you have done and are continuing to do!

Dr. Martin Luther King Jr. January 15, 1929 – April 4, 1968

Sojourner Truth 1797-November 26, 1883

Frederick Douglass February 1818 – February 20, 1895

Harriet Tubman March 1822-March 10, 1913

W. E. B. Du Bois February 23, 1868 – August 27, 1963

Dorothy Height March 24, 1912 – April 20, 2010

Rosa Parks February 4, 1913 – October 24, 2005

Jackie Robinson January 31, 1919- October 24, 1972

Maya Angelou April 4, 1928-May 28, 2014

John Lewis February 21, 1940 – July 17, 2020

Chadwick Boseman November 29, 1976 - August 28, 2020

Al Sharpton October 3, 1954

Oprah Winfrey January 29, 1954

LeBron James December 30, 1984

Judge Maurice Mosley June 4, 1946

Congress Women Jahana Hayes March 8, 1973

Jason Burger my 6th grade English teacher

Michelle Obama January 17, 1964

President Barack Obama August 4, 1961

My grandmother Patricia "MEMA" Williams

July 20, 1951- May 23, 2014

Lastly to my BIGGEST hero,

my daddy, Lance Christopher Williams

I love you, thank you for giving me life

July 28, 1983-July 6, 2008

One Sunday morning, Mom woke up me and my little sister Brooklyn.

My name's London by the way.

She said,
"Girls, we are going to attend a PROTEST".

"A protest!" Brooklyn cried,
"What's a protest Mommy?"

Mom explained:

"A protest is when a lot of people come together to show others that they strongly dislike or are against an idea or event. For example, some people protest about racism or war. Today, we are protesting about racism."

"I learned about that in school,
that people have different skin colors.
And sometimes people don't like those who
are different from them and that's wrong."

"Like what Claudette Colvin went through when she was fighing for our civil rights. On March 2, 1955, she was arrested at the age of 15 in Montgomery, Alabama for refusing to give up her seat on a crowded, segregated bus." I said.

"That's right London, it's very wrong and we are STILL fighting for our rights."
Said Mom.

"Mommy, can we make signs?"
I asked.

"Sure, what will they say?"

"How about BLACK LIVES MATTER?
Or one that I've been hearing on TV
lately: 'I can't breathe'."

"Those will be great, Mom said."
Then we took our face masks and left
the house for the protest.

"At the protest there were HUNDREDS of people of all races, marching together..."

"...everyone was united. Well, most of the time. Some people were really angry. It was a little scary and I even cried."

"The crowds of protestors were being led through our city by police officers, and they were riding on horses."

Everyone shouted "No Justice! No Peace!"

Me and Brooklyn marched with the crowds, held up our signs, and we too shouted No Justice! No Peace!"

It felt great to know that we were a part of making history.

We were a part of changing the world.

We attended
Our 1st Protest!

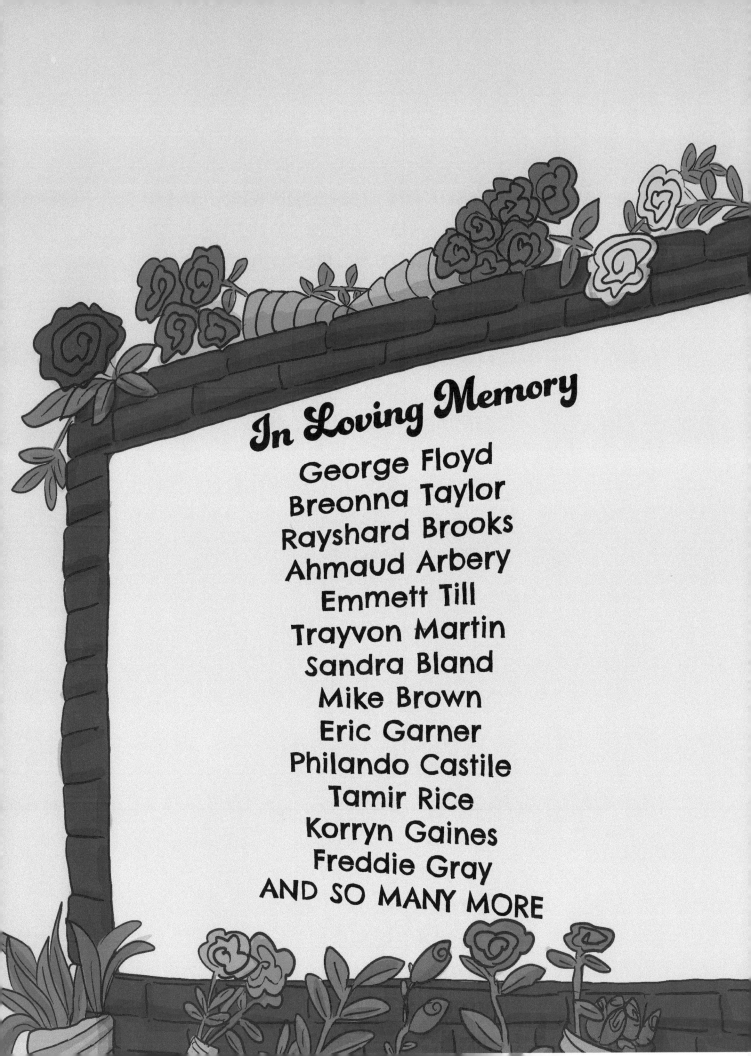

In Loving Memory

George Floyd
Breonna Taylor
Rayshard Brooks
Ahmaud Arbery
Emmett Till
Trayvon Martin
Sandra Bland
Mike Brown
Eric Garner
Philando Castile
Tamir Rice
Korryn Gaines
Freddie Gray
AND SO MANY MORE

A message from Mommy:

To my beautiful melanin daughters.
I pray you know just how much I love you,
how proud I am to be your mother.
Nothing in this world could be
as beautiful as you, to me.
I pray that you follow in the footsteps of our
dear Lord as you walk through life each day.
Chase your dreams and reach for the stars.
Never forget how worthy you are, for you are
QUEENS. Always know that next to God, you
have me and I will ALWAYS be here for you.

Love Mommy

Our 1st Protest is not affiliated with the
Black Lives Matter Organization